WHICH WAY
America?

**What the Bible says about
where we're going...**

Mark Finley
and **Steven Mosley**

Pacific Press® Publish
Nampa, I
Oshawa, Ontari

98 99 00 01 02 • 5 4

ISB

Edited by Kenneth R. Wade
Cover by Palimor Studios

Copyright © 1998 by
Pacific Press® Publishing Association
Printed in the United States of America
All Rights Reserved

Unless otherwise noted, all Bible texts are quoted from
the New King James Version.

N 0-8163-1693-7

3 2 1

Contents

Chapter 1

Freedom and the Lamb

It began among thatched-roof houses between the Atlantic Ocean and a vast wilderness. It began in a settlement hurriedly built in the territory of the Powhatan people. This is where the great American experiment began. The colonists called it Jamestown in honor of their king. It was to become the first permanent English settlement in North America.

The people of Jamestown would have an incredibly hard time maintaining their toehold in the New World. They barely survived those first few harsh winters. They came close to starving to death many times. The Indians whose country they'd invaded sometimes fought back. Their numbers dwindled.

But something very powerful kept these American forefathers from giving up and sailing back to England. Something very powerful had moved them to forsake their homes, sail across the stormy Atlantic, and try to create a civilization from scratch, from the raw materials of an unknown continent.

There is a structure that dates back to the original Jamestown settlement. It's the tower of a church built in the 1640s, now part of the Memorial Church built in 1907.

After the colonists had constructed some fortifications and arranged for temporary shelters, their primary concern was to provide a place in which they could worship God. They built a church.

Longing for freedom

It was a longing for freedom that propelled the settlement of the New World. But not just any freedom. It was the desire to worship God freely, as conscience dictated—without interference. It was the desire to escape religious persecution.

Yes, there were some adventurers among the Jamestown colonists. There were some who just wanted to make their fortune in the New World. But among the colonists landing at Plymouth Rock or Chesapeake Bay or Cape Henry, it was chiefly the desire for religious freedom that burned in their hearts. That's why they could endure incredible hardships. That's why they wanted to build a new civilization from scratch.

Imagine what it must have been like setting out across the vast Atlantic in boats like the *Susan Constant*, the *Godspeed*, and the *Discovery*. Imagine what it must have been like being tossed about by mid-ocean storms in boats like these.

We get a close-up look at what the colonists endured in the records left to us by those aboard the original Mayflower. That's the ship that brought the Pilgrims to Plymouth Rock. We hear of storms that almost tore the boat apart. Rough seas splashed into the ship at one point and extinguished the galley fires. The Pilgrims had no heat for cooking after that. They stayed wet and cold most of the time. Many became sick. Crude seamen on the Mayflower took out their frustrations by tormenting the Pilgrims—many of whom wondered if they'd ever see land again.

But there's something else that stands out in the record of the Mayflower crossing. And that is the Pilgrim worship services. These people praised God. They worshiped in fair weather and foul. They worshiped in sickness and health. They worshiped in joy and in despair.

Everyone is familiar with the picture of the Pilgrims kneeling on Plymouth Rock and giving thanks to God after landing safely. But these people had been falling on their knees all along. That's how they lived their lives. That's what drove them across the ocean. That's what enabled them to endure so much—the dream of religious freedom.

The Pilgrims were really taking a journey away from centuries of religious persecution in Europe. They were hoping to put an ocean between them and a long, bloody tradition of intolerance.

Peaceful, Bible-believing Christians had been hunted down, arrested, imprisoned, burned, or sold as galley slaves—simply because they disagreed with the established church.

In the 1400s and 1500s, people like the Hussites, the Huguenots, the Lollards, the Anabaptists, and the Waldensians suffered greatly because they chose to "Obey God rather than men." They would not conform to traditions they believed contrary to the Bible.

And religious intolerance was still the norm when the Pilgrims set sail. William Brewster, the man who pastored the group embarking on the Mayflower, had to be smuggled on board the ship. The authorities were trying to arrest him. Brewster had dared to criticize the established Church of England in print.

These Puritans, these religious dissenters, wanted to be able to express their convictions without fear of oppression. They wanted to be able to share their faith freely.

Interestingly enough, one of the items they brought aboard the Mayflower was a large iron press. They intended to print religious pamphlets in the new colony. And that press came into good use—quite unexpectedly during the Atlantic crossing. After a fierce storm, one of the main beams in the middle of the ship began to bow and crack. The crew feared the Mayflower would break up. There seemed to be no way to repair the beam.

But the Pilgrim passengers remembered their press. It had two strong iron plates that could be pulled together by a large screw. The pilgrims used this to jack up the main beam and slip a solid post underneath it. With this as a foundation, the Mayflower made it to Plymouth Rock.

A divine mission

You know, the faith of the Pilgrims was a lot like that central beam that held the Mayflower together. These people believed they were on a divine mission. They wanted to become a "light set on a hill." That gave them stability. They made it through one hardship after another because they believed they were part of God's big plan.

Those who came here to create a New World looked at the whole world from God's perspective, from the Bible's perspective. And the Bible actually unveils for us the great drama of religious intolerance versus the struggle for religious freedom.

Take a look at Revelation, chapter 12. In verse one, we see God's pure church pictured as a woman clothed with the sun who wears a crown of twelve stars. An adversary appears in verse three—a great red dragon with seven heads and seven crowns. This dragon symbolizes Satan.

He sweeps a third of the stars from heaven and casts them to earth. That is a reference to the angels who rebelled with Satan in heaven and were exiled to earth.

In this same chapter, the pure woman is about to give birth to a child. And this dragon stands ready to devour her child as soon as it is born. This refers to Jesus Christ, born from God's chosen people. He is the One who proclaimed "liberty to the captives," the One who "let the oppressed go free."

Satan wants to destroy Him, the author of liberty. And he tried to do that through King Herod's massacre. As soon as Herod heard that the Christ had been born in Bethlehem, he had every male infant in that town killed.

Satan, the dragon, continues his war against Christ by continuing to attack God's people. "the dragon . . . persecuted the woman who gave birth to the male Child" (Revelation 12:13).

Satan is the author of religious intolerance. He is behind religious persecution.

Christ came to set human beings free. The heart of Jesus' ministry is set forth in these words: "And you shall know the truth, and the truth shall make you free" (John 8:32).

Satan is determined to keep people oppressed. That's the reason religious tyranny is so diabolical. That's the reason love and intolerance have clashed so fiercely down through the centuries.

Revelation 12 also pictures for us God's coming to the rescue of His persecuted people. "But the woman was given two wings of a great eagle, that she might fly into the wilderness to her place, where she is nourished for a time" (Revelation 12:14).

Revelation 12:6 echoes this thought, telling us the woman flees to the wilderness, to a place prepared by God, and is sustained there.

Down through the years, various groups of believers were forced to meet in remote mountain caves or deep in the forest. They nourished their faith in these secret places.

But Pilgrim believers, perhaps more than anyone else, truly did flee into a wilderness, the vast wilderness of America. And they believed this place had been prepared for them by God. Here they could build a new society of faith to His glory.

Intolerance continues

Unfortunately, that new society still carried something of the Old World with it. Throughout the colonies, stocks stood in the public square of most colonial towns. They were used not just to punish drunkenness or petty theft, but also to punish people for missing church.

The Puritans rejected the creeds of the medieval church. But they weren't completely free of her spirit of intolerance. They very much wanted to practice their religion without interference. But they were quite willing to interfere with others who wanted to believe differently.

The Puritans wanted to create a righteous community so badly that they began to legislate it. They established mandatory religious observances for all colonists. People who missed church too often could be placed in stocks. People who tripped up over some rule about Sunday observance could be humiliated.

Officials of the established church could be even more tyrannical. Sir William Berkeley, one of the early governors of Virginia, wanted to keep the colony safe for the Church of England. He tried to drive out all Quakers. Some members of this peace-loving sect were arrested and imprisoned. One of them, a man named George Wilson, managed to get letters out describing what he and fellow believers were going through. They were chained in a filthy dungeon in Jamestown, almost suffocating in the stench of their own filth. Wilson would eventually die in irons.

It's clear that the desire for freedom had populated the New World. But the New World was not always so free. People came here to defend their right to believe as conscience dictated. But they did not always defend the right of others to believe differently.

It would take a very special man to blaze the trail of pure religious liberty in the American wilderness.

Roger Williams arrived in the New World eleven years after the Pilgrims landed at Plymouth Rock. He saw what few of his contemporaries had seen: that religious freedom is a God-given right of all, whatever their creed.

Williams began to speak out in the Massachusetts Bay Colony against a tax-supported clergy. No one, he maintained, should have to support a church "against his own consent."

His opponents were scandalized. "What! Is not the laborer worthy of his hire?" they asked.

"Yes," Williams shot back, "from them that hire him."

Roger Williams was banished from Massachusetts. He found refuge among the Indians. Williams had always tried to protect them from exploitation, and Native Americans had come to trust him. Under his guidance many Indians from various tribes became Christians.

A place for freedom

Eventually, Roger Williams would create a place of refuge in the New World. He bought some land at a fair price from the Naragansett people and established the little colony of Rhode Island.

Its royal charter of 1663 stated this: "No person within the said colony . . . shall be in any wise molested, punished, disquieted or called in question, for any differences in opinion in matters of religion."

Williams was the first person in modern Christendom to establish civil government on the basis of liberty of conscience. He offered a haven of protection for Jews, Quakers, Catholics, Seventh Day Baptists, and others who were rejected in both Europe and the New England colonies.

Rhode Island became a refuge for the oppressed. And Rhode Island prospered. Its foundation principles—civil and religious liberty—would become the cornerstones of the American Republic.

Here at the very beginning of the great American experiment we had two very different views of the church, two very different views of religion. We had people like Sir William Berkeley who tried to drive out non-Anglicans from Virginia. He thought this would make the church strong.

And we had Roger Williams who created Rhode Island for liberty of conscience. He felt that was the only way real Christianity could flourish.

It makes us wonder. What made the difference? What pushes some toward intolerance—and others toward protecting religious freedom? Why are some driven to control conscience—and others motivated to set it free?

I believe Roger Williams himself gives us an important answer. As an old man, looking back on his life, he pointed to the one thing that had shaped him the most. More than sixty years before he wrote, "The Father of Lights and Mercies touched my Soul with a love to himself."

Roger Williams had experienced grace. Mercy had touched his soul. He knew what it was like for a sinful human being to be accepted by a holy God. He'd experienced salvation as a gift.

Roger Williams had been drawn to God by love. Love had won him over. And that's how he related to other people.

God doesn't coerce. God draws us to Himself with cords of love. So why should we coerce other people?

You can see grace in this man's life in the way he tried to console his wife Mary during a crisis. She was suffering from a serious illness and, in her depression, she began to doubt her acceptance by God as His child.

Williams wrote her a very long letter of comfort and assurance. He went to great lengths to select Bible passages that would encourage her. And he offered them, he said, as a bouquet, "a little posy," to the one he called "My Dearest Love and Companion."

This man knew how to comfort. This man knew he was loved by God.

I believe that's the secret to his courageous stand for religious liberty. He didn't have to control others. He didn't have to force anyone to believe as he did. God had won Him over by love and that's how he expected others to be won over.

As I mentioned earlier, passages in Revelation show us the great drama of religious intolerance versus the struggle for religious freedom. It shows us earthly powers trying to oppress God's people.

But do you know what other symbol dominates the book of Revelation? The Lamb of God—Jesus Christ. The Lamb of God sacrificed for our sins. He's at the center of the drama.

Worship in heaven

Revelation 5 gives us a vivid picture of worship in heaven. Who is at the center of praise? The Lamb. The heavenly host can't stop declaring, "Worthy is the Lamb who was slain."

Chapter 7 shows us a picture of the redeemed, a great multitude from every nation. What are they doing? Waving palm branches before the Lamb of God.

Chapter 13 shows us a terrible beast who blasphemes against God and who demands human worship. But in contrast we read of "the Lamb slain from the foundation of the world." The beast coerces. The Lamb lays down His life.

Chapter 17 pictures oppressive, corrupt religion as Babylon, the Mother of Harlots. Who overcomes Babylon? The Lamb—the chosen and faithful Lamb of God.

And finally, when Revelation pictures the glorious re-union of God and His people in heaven, it's called the wedding supper of the Lamb.

The Lamb is at the center of the drama. He's the one who can stand against tyranny and oppression.

Friends, do you know what genuine religious liberty is based on? It's based on the sacrificial love of Jesus Christ. It's based on this Lamb of God who gave Himself up for the sins of the world.

God committed Himself to winning us over through love, not coercion. That's what this Lamb is saying to us in the book of Revelation.

And people who don't understand that love don't understand religious freedom. People who are not moved by grace are moved by something else. Human nature moves us to something else.

Without grace, we naturally want to control other people.

Without love, we naturally have to make other people think we're right.

Without the Lamb of God, religion becomes oppressive and human beings turn into beasts.

There's a story that comes to us from the early Jamestown settlement that gives us a beautiful picture of grace. It's the story of Pocahontas and John Smith—the real story.

Tensions between the colonists and the Indians who occupied this land kept mounting. John Smith, a courageous leader of the settlers, tried to negotiate peace with the Native American, King Powhatan.

But one day, during an Indian ceremony, Smith was seized by warriors who forced his head down on some rocks. They raised their clubs as if to kill him.

Suddenly, the king's favorite daughter, a young girl named Pocahontas, rushed from the crowd and laid herself over the captive. She offered her life in exchange for Smith's. The execution was halted.

Two days later, Smith was astonished to learn that he'd been adopted as the king's honored son.

Afterward, Pocahontas devoted her brief life to promoting harmony between her people and the white people. Sometimes only her gifts of food kept the starving colonists alive. Sometimes she had to defy her angry father. But Pocahontas, more than anyone else, sustained the uneasy peace in this part of the New World.

She eventually fell in love with and married an English farmer named John Rolfe. He was a Christian man of kindness and integrity. Pocahontas began studying the Bible and soon adopted the Christian faith, becoming a believer in the Lamb of God who takes away the sin of the world.

She understood what sacrifice means. She understood what giving yourself away means.

Have you made that discovery? Have you encountered the love of God that can set you free? Or are you still trying to control other people?

We can only stop controlling other people if we are free ourselves. We can only draw other people with love if we are loved ourselves.

God wants to create a New World inside us, a new creation. But it has to be built on a foundation of love. Every other foundation will fail.

We need the Lamb of God who takes away the sins of the world. We need His grace to fill our lives. Let's start building on that foundation right away.

Chapter 2

Facing the Crisis

Fourteen-year-old hookers on Sunset Boulevard. Parents who abandon their babies in dumpsters. Skinheads and racist cults. Separatist groups shooting it out with government agents. Abortion on demand. Children abused and neglected. Pornography reaching our children on the Internet. Churches bombed.

People are starting to wonder—is this America? Has "the land of the free and the home of the brave" come to this?

These are the faces that remind us of America in a time of crisis. They are the weary, anxious, but alert faces of soldiers out on patrol. At the Korean War Memorial they cross a slope, gray and ghostlike, a little larger than life.

They remind us of a time when communism seemed to be sweeping over much of the globe. Country after country was falling under the rule of tyranny.

And soldiers like these tried to make a stand on the cold, muddy hills of a beleaguered country far, far away.

At the Vietnam Veterans Memorial we see names that remind us of the cost of times of crisis. America wanted to come to the rescue of yet another nation that seemed the victim of communist aggression. We wanted to widen the circle of freedom.

There are more than 58,000 names on the dark granite walls of the Vietnam Veterans Memorial. It was a very long war that wore us down. It made us doubt ourselves.

But standing there, looking at all those names, you are compelled to believe that the sacrifice was meaningful. That these soldiers and their country were fighting for more than just self-interest. That they really did go on a mission to advance the cause of freedom. That, at the very least, America rose and faced a time of crisis.

A different kind of war

Today, we're facing a crisis of a very different kind. A war is raging right here in our land, not just in some trouble spot far away. It's a war against decency and morality, a war against the values that make a nation and a people worthy of respect.

And the question is—are we going to face this crisis? Are we going to stand up and meet it head-on and be willing to make sacrifices? Are we willing to put our names on the line?

Let's take a closer look at just why our nation is in such trouble today. And then let's look for the solution. It will help us, first of all, to get a look at where we've come from.

The Jefferson Memorial is quite an imposing monument to one of the founders of the American Republic. Walking between the classic columns of this monument, you are humbled by the vision of this man who worked so hard to make America truly democratic, truly the land of the free.

"All men are endowed by their Creator with certain inalienable rights," he wrote. These are words that changed history.

And there on those walls we find words from Thomas Jefferson that are a little less familiar. But I believe they suggest what lay behind the ideals of the founding fathers.

"I tremble for my country when I reflect that God is just."

A simple statement. But it speaks volumes about this man's perspective and his worldview. Jefferson had a strong sense of God's justice and our moral obligation to a holy God. And when he looked around and saw cruelty and corruption—he had to tremble.

Jefferson, in fact, was not a completely orthodox Christian, partly because he'd seen so much misuse of religion by people calling themselves Christians. But he and the other founding fathers shared a profound awareness of our moral duty to God. It was deeply ingrained in these men.

Jefferson called the moral system of Jesus, "the most perfect and sublime that has ever been taught." And he admired Christ most of all because, "He pushed his scrutinies into the heart of man; erected his tribunal in the region of his thoughts, and purified the waters at the fountainhead."

In other words, Jesus made His principles sink into the heart and change human beings from the inside out. Jesus made people righteous.

Yes, when Thomas Jefferson reflected that God is just, he had to tremble for his country.

It's my conviction that we've lost that strong sense of our moral obligation to God as a people. That's what's missing. We don't tremble anymore; we shrug things off. We don't call ourselves to account anymore. We make excuses.

I believe we find a mirror of our times in certain Bible passages that describe earth's final days. Jesus listed various signs of the end in Matthew 24. "And because lawlessness will abound, the love of many will grow cold" (Matthew 24:12).

A new kind of lawlessness

Today, lawlessness is abounding in a completely new way. It's not just the crime that plagues our cities—the gangs and drug lords and embezzlers. That's the symptom of a problem that's eating away at us inside. Lawlessness has seeped down into our hearts. That's the great peril and the crisis we're facing.

The law doesn't stand above us anymore. We don't feel that sense of moral obligation to an absolute standard. We can make up the rules ourselves. We can just do "what's right for me."

This kind of thinking has been seeping into us for decades. And now, finally, moral demands have been swallowed up by selfishness. What is right has collapsed into what I want.

That's the kind of lawlessness that's so dangerous.

And what happens as a result? The love of human beings grows cold. The most basic human bonds are no longer holding. Families are torn apart in the cruelest of ways. We hear horrifying stories of children neglected and abused and molested by their parents. The most innocent among us are being brutalized every day. We're becoming a nation of scarred survivors.

Yes, the love of many has grown cold. There's less and less restraint on the evil in the human heart.

The Apostle Paul expanded on this picture in 2 Timothy. Again this is a picture of the *end times* that mirrors our times: "But know this, that in the last days perilous times will come: for men will be lovers of themselves, lovers of money, boasters, proud, blasphemers, disobedient to parents, unthankful, unholy, unloving, unforgiving, slanderers without self-control, brutal, despisers of good, traitors, headstrong, haughty, lovers of pleasure rather than lovers of God, having a form of godliness but denying its power" (2 Timothy 3:1-5).

Please note that this is not just a description of crime in the streets. It zeroes in on the real problem. It's talking about character issues and about people being corrupted from the inside out.

People start loving money more than God. Materialism swallows up spirituality.

People grow haughty and headstrong. They no longer reverence the good.

People pay lip service to religion, but deny its moral power in their lives.

Yes, lawlessness is abounding. It has seeped down into our hearts. We may pay lip service to what's right and wrong, to God's principles. But there's a very different principle working inside us; something that drives us in a different direction.

Internalizing the law

On July 11, 1804, the vice-president of the United States, Aaron Burr, decided to settle his differences with Alexander Hamilton by challenging him to a duel. The two men had developed quite a bitter rivalry. It was political. And it was personal.

Hamilton accepted the challenge. The two men met on the Jersey Palisades overlooking the Hudson River in New York State.

Aaron Burr fired a bullet that cut through his rival's liver and spine. Hamilton died after 30 hours of agony.

Interestingly enough, dueling had already been declared illegal in New York. Even offering or receiving a challenge to duel was against the law.

But most ironic of all, Alexander Hamilton himself had helped in the effort to pass this ban on dueling. He'd argued for it. He'd helped put it on the books. But that law hadn't become a big enough principle in his own life. It wasn't big enough to save him in a time of crisis.

Paul talks about the law working inside us that wars against the law of God. It's our human nature. It calls to us very loudly. And usually we give in to its demands.

That's why it's so vital that we hear a higher calling in our lives—away from lawlessness. God's voice must ring out clearly in our hearts. God's moral principles have to become very real.

Some of us are inclined to see God's moral law, or any laws for that matter, as annoyances, something that interferes with our freedom.

Take Mike, for example. He had no use for any laws. And he especially resented all the rules that governed driving on the road. Traffic laws irritated him. "They're for sissies and grannies," he told himself.

Mike speeded everywhere he went. And he was lucky. He seldom got a ticket more than once a year. And he often beat those tickets in court.

Then one day, after a couple of drinks at a bar, Mike set out in a great hurry to go nowhere in particular. He whizzed through a school zone at forty-five miles an hour.

A little girl was just then crossing the street. Six-year-old Jennifer arced through the air, leaving her shoes behind on the pavement.

For days, her life hung in the balance at a county hospital. Night after night, her parents kept up a desperate prayer vigil. Fortunately, Jennifer survived, but her recovery was slow and painful.

Afterwards, Mike would never look at traffic laws in the same way. He realized they weren't silly rules; they protected people. And if he'd obeyed them they could have protected a child from a great deal of pain and terror.

God's purpose for us

The law of God was meant to protect us, to create a place of safety for us. But that law must sink into our hearts.

The prophets of Israel tried over and over to make the voice of God compelling for their contemporaries. They tried to make "thus saith the Lord" a guide in their lives. And they tried to awaken Israel to a sense of its high calling.

Here's God speaking to His people in Exodus: "You

have seen . . . how I bore you on eagles' wings and brought you to Myself. Now therefore, if you will indeed obey My voice and keep My covenant, then you shall be a special treasure to me above all people; for all the earth is Mine. And you shall be to Me a kingdom of priests and a holy nation. . . ." (Exodus 19:4-6).

God had wonderful plans for Israel. He wanted them to be a kingdom of priests who would shed His light to the whole world. He wanted them to become a holy nation, a special treasure.

And how would that happen? Only if they listened to God, only if they obeyed His voice and kept the covenant.

Israel could become a great nation by becoming sensitive to its moral obligations to God. It would fall apart if it shied away from its moral obligations.

Eventually, Israel took the wrong road. They were seduced by the idolatry and immorality of their neighbors. They stopped listening to God's voice.

The prophet Jeremiah lamented Israel's downfall. You can feel God's heart breaking as he declares in Jeremiah, "Be astonished, O heavens . . . For My people have committed two evils: they have forsaken Me, the fountain of living waters, and hewn themselves cisterns—broken cisterns that can hold no water" (Jeremiah 2:12, 13).

Israel would be conquered by Babylon, Jerusalem burned and its citizens taken off into exile.

Why? Because they lost their calling. They turned away from the source of life, the fountain of living water, and they ended up with broken, dry wells, the moral life drained out of them.

That was a great tragedy. It's a tragedy that God would like America to avoid. Our founding fathers wanted this country to be a "city set on a hill" like Israel. They dreamed of a place where God would be honored and all men would be free.

But that dream is in danger of dying. We've stopped looking up. And our wells are running dry. The moral life is draining out of America.

Facing the crisis

This country faced a grave crisis during the presidency of Abraham Lincoln. The issue that was tearing America apart was slavery. Southern states were threatening to secede from the Union if the slaves were freed. They argued that their entire economy, their whole way of life, depended on slave labor.

Lincoln wanted more than anything else to preserve the Union. He was a reconciler, a bridge builder. He tried to do everything he could to prevent his country from being torn apart by the Civil War. "United we stand, divided we fall."

But there was another principle at stake, what Lincoln called the "monstrous injustice of slavery." He once said, "If slavery is not wrong, nothing is wrong. I can not remember when I did not so think, and feel."

Human beings owning other human beings just wasn't right. No matter how many people thought it was OK—no matter how much the country's economy was tied to it. No matter what people threatened to do if slavery ended. It still was wrong. It was immoral.

And so, after much agony, Abraham Lincoln finally issued the Emancipation Proclamation. As President of the United States of America, he freed the slaves. Lincoln faced the crisis, and he made a stand. With that proclamation, America took a giant step toward truly becoming the land of the free.

You can't visit the Lincoln Memorial, or the Jefferson Memorial, without sensing the power of these men's beliefs and convictions. Their monuments are about great ideals. The pillars and domes and facades of stone enshrine principles that made these men great. They weren't just living for themselves; they weren't just making up the rules as they went along. They felt an awesome sense of moral obligation to a holy God. They poured their life's energy into trying to do the right thing.

We have to recover that passion. We have to recover that sense of a high calling. We have to know, as King Solomon knew, that it is righteousness that exalts a nation.

We're lost without it. Our moral world has been shrinking for some time. Lawlessness has been seeping deep into our hearts.

We have to take a stand again. We have to face the crisis. We have to make the hard decisions.

Have you discovered something that's bigger than you? Have you discovered something that can give a shape to your life?

We can't go on living without the law—in our hearts. We can't go on pretending that right and wrong are just what I like and don't like. Morality is bigger than that.

Is God's Word bigger than you? You have to decide that in your own mind. Are you going to really listen to God? Are you going to be taught by Him? Or will you let in only what you're comfortable with?

God's Word, God's moral voice, has to be bigger than our desires and opinions and bigger than our prejudices.

Have you found principles you can base your life on? Do you understand the ideals that Jesus turned into flesh and blood on this earth? Has He "erected His tribunal" in your thoughts, as Thomas Jefferson put it? Has He pushed His scrutinies into your heart? Has He "purified the waters at the fountainhead?"

Jesus calls us to take responsibility for our moral selves, no excuses.

He calls us to find our happiness by working for the happiness of others. To speak the truth in love, even when it's unwelcome.

He calls us to be gracious to the ungracious and to oppose tyranny and confront those who abuse.

He calls us to honor the needs of others in all our relationships.

Have you heard that calling? Is God's moral voice echoing in your heart? We desperately need those ideals in our lives today. Our moral world is shrinking. We need something to expand us before our world collapses altogether.

I ask you to respond to God's higher calling today. He calls you to a renewal of Christian ideals. And those ideals can only be nurtured in an honest relationship with Christ. So I urge you to begin listening to Him each day. Spend time in God's Word; become sensitive to His voice. Open up your life to His guidance.

That's how you discover something bigger than yourself, something you can build your life on.

Chapter 3

Making America Godly

Williamsburg, Virginia is a window back in time. This carefully reconstructed town gives us a glimpse of life in colonial days. In the 1700s, Williamsburg served as the capitol of the Virginia Colony.

And it was there, in the Capitol building, that Virginia legislators first hammered out the foundation for the American Republic. The legislators included men like George Washington, Thomas Jefferson, Patrick Henry, and James Madison.

When he was 14, Madison had an experience in his hometown in Orange County, Virginia that left a lasting impression. He was walking down a street toward the town square one day and noticed a large crowd gathering.

He worked his way to the front. A man was speaking to the people from the barred window of a jail cell. He had a kind, noble face, and preached a powerful gospel sermon that deeply moved young James Madison. He'd seldom heard any minister preach with such conviction.

So he asked a bystander, "Why is he in jail?"

The man replied. "He's one of those Baptist ministers. They're not licensed to preach here in Virginia."

Madison felt hot with indignation. Jailed for preaching? How could his beloved Virginia jail men for proclaiming the gospel!

Madison knew his Bible. He knew about Peter's bold declaration before Jewish authorities: "We must obey God rather than men!"

And at that moment a great passion began to build in the heart of this young man. It was a passion that would someday make him a champion of human rights and the father of the American constitution.

The capitol building in Williamsburg was known as the House of Burgesses in pre-Revolutionary times. Here, Virginia's elected representatives met twice a year to manage the colony and pass legislation.

James Madison served for a time as one of those Burgesses. Initially, he'd wanted to become a minister. He'd studied theology and biblical languages at the College of New Jersey—now Princeton University.

But when Madison finished college, America was taking rapid strides toward independence. A new spirit was electrifying the air. And he wanted to help his country become a free republic.

When he arrived at the Virginia House of Burgesses, Madison learned that a group of Baptists in a nearby county had been imprisoned for expressing religious views different from those of the established church, the Church of England. He was shocked. He went to see these people and promised, "I shall not be silent."

True to his word, Madison became an outspoken critic of intolerance and persecution.

As revolutionary momentum grew, the Virginia legislators drafted their own state declaration of independence. Madison co-authored the Virginia Declaration of Rights. That document stated: "Religion or the duty which we owe our Creator and the manner of discharging it can be directed only by reason and conviction, not by force or violence."

Not all the legislators wanted to champion religious liberty, however. There were other forces in the Virginia Colony that worked to enforce certain religious practices. Those forces often gathered at the Governor's Palace in Williamsburg.

Ladies and gentlemen in splendid dress often strolled through the gardens. The governors liked to give elegant balls and entertainments on special occasions, occasions like the anniversary of the English King's accession to the throne.

The Old World found a courtly echo at the Governor's Palace. It seemed only natural for the early governors of Virginia to try to establish a state religion, to make the Church of England the official church of the colony.

And it even seemed right to them to try to cleanse Virginia from what they regarded as pestilential sects: Baptists, Quakers, Catholics. Members of these religions were often exiled from Virginia.

This attitude persisted even in America's revolutionary days when everyone was waving the banner of liberty and independence. During Virginia's revolutionary convention, James Madison argued that Virginia should go beyond just toleration of various religions. It should affirm, he said, the "equal and unalienable right" to freedom of religion and disestablishment of official state religion.

Madison couldn't get his colleagues to go that far. But he did manage to get these words into the colony's Declaration of Rights: "All men are equally entitled to the free exercise of religion."

Later, after America became independent, leaders in Virginia still wanted to raise taxes to support Christian ministers. That seemed harmless enough. Taxes would be used to support clergymen of all denominations.

But Madison clearly saw the danger of having the state finance the church. In 1785, he wrote a "Memorial and Remonstrance Against Religious Assessments." As a committed Christian, Madison penned these words:

"While we assert for ourselves a freedom to embrace, to profess, and to observe the religion which we believe to be of divine origin, we cannot deny an equal freedom to those whose minds have not yet yielded to the evidence which has convinced us. If this freedom be abused, it is an offense against God."

Madison wanted to spread the Christian religion. He believed it was "of divine origin." But people had to be free to accept or reject the claims of Christ—without any coercion from the state. Freedom of religion means a freedom to believe as well as a freedom *not* to believe.

Thankfully, James Madison and others like him made the separation of church and state a founding principle of the American Republic. Religious freedom has flourished in America.

Jesus and the government

But perhaps a more important issue is what the founder of Christianity had to say about this matter.

How did Jesus say His church should be established?

On one occasion, the Pharisees tried to entrap Jesus with a question about paying taxes to Caesar, the oppressor of the Jews.

Jesus asked them to show him a tax coin. Then he asked whose image and inscription was on it.

They had to reply, "Caesar's."

So Jesus gave them His answer, found in Matthew 22: "Render therefore to Caesar the things that are Caesar's, and to God the things that are God's" (verse 21).

Here Christ asserted that church and state have separate spheres of authority. He realized what His disciples were slow to understand—that when religion is armed with political power, it becomes coercive and intolerant. It destroys the true gospel.

In Christ's day, human beings were subject to rulers with absolute authority. Few individuals could live freely according to their personal convictions.

But Christ established His kingdom on different principles. He called people not to subjection, but to service. He, as the Master, became the servant. He showed us how to exercise authority in spiritual matters. He bore His disciples' burdens. He shared their poverty and practiced self-denial. He healed the sick and welcomed the outcast. And He asked only for a voluntary response, a free allegiance motivated by love.

At Jesus' trial, Pilate wondered why the Jews had brought this Man before him. Jesus answered, "My kingdom is not of this world. If My kingdom were of this world, My servants would fight, so that I should not be delivered to the Jews" (John 18:36).

Force was not a part of Christ's program. Once the disciples wanted to punish some Samaritans for rejecting their Master. Jesus told them, "You do not know what manner of spirit you are of."

Jesus exercised an extraordinary, miraculous power during His short stay on this earth. But He never once exercised it to punish someone who rejected Him. Jesus refused all political power. On one occasion a large crowd tried to seize Him and crown Him their king by force. But Jesus escaped across the Sea of Galilee.

What would have happened if Jesus had become that kind of king? Have you ever wondered? Couldn't He have stamped out all kinds of social and political evils? Couldn't He have done a lot more?

The simple answer is, no. Christ's revolution went deeper than government reform. He turned the world upside down in a more profound way.

Real change is change that happens in the human heart. To be efficient, the cure must transform the human heart. And that's where the power of Christ's kingdom lies. Listen to how John describes it: "But as many as received Him, to them He gave the right to become children of God, even to those who believe in His name: who were born, not . . . of the will of man, but of God" (John 1:12, 13).

People are transformed when they become children of God. And children of God are the ones who transform society.

That's what the Kingdom of Heaven is all about. That's what Christ's church is all about. And this transformation is a spiritual process. It can only happen when human beings freely respond to the love of God. It can only happen if the conscience is left unshackled. It can only happen when the Holy Spirit gets through to the heart.

And I'm afraid that, as America rushes toward the year 2000, we are losing sight of this vital principle. Many Christians are focusing on a different type of transformation.

Legislating morality

Washington, D. C. is the center of political power in the United States. It's where the nation's laws are made and interpreted and enforced. And it's where many Christians have come—to try to change America.

Political action groups with a Christian agenda have become the power to reckon with in Washington. Ministers are mobilizing churches to promote a new strategy—the "Christianizing" of America through political activism.

Believers see their country drowning in immorality. The forces of vice and corruption seem so strong. The church seems so weak. And so they want to turn back the tide. They want Christian values to be honored again in America.

And so they've made the church more politically sophisticated. Christians know how to get their agenda into the legislature now. They know how to pressure political candidates. They know how to lobby and raise money and mobilize voters.

Now please, let me be very clear on what the problems are with this new activism. The problem is *not* that Christians are getting into government. The problem is *not* that Christians are politically active. Christians have the right to influence our government just as much as anyone else. Christians have the duty to work for just laws and policies in our society.

The problem arises when we try to defeat ungodliness through legislation. The problem arises when we try to enforce morality through government policy.

We do need government to restrain evil. Murderers and rapists and embezzlers need to be restrained by force. But government *cannot* enforce godliness, personal morality.

Government can prevent us from being bad—to a certain extent. But it cannot make us good.

This is what the church must realize today. Government can't make us good. Only Jesus Christ can make us good. Spiritual renewal doesn't happen as an act of Congress. Revival doesn't happen because we push the right laws through.

Washington isn't the answer for the church today. But many Christians have come here looking for answers to spiritual problems. And there is great danger when church and state join forces. We may like to think they are joining forces for good. But the result of that union has always been a disaster.

Problems prophesied

I believe it would help us all to recapture a certain vision from the Bible, a certain perspective from its last book. The Revelation. Amazingly enough, the recent shift in the thinking of Christians in this country parallels a prediction in Bible prophecy.

"Then I saw another beast coming up out of the earth, and he had two horns like a lamb and spoke like a dragon. And he exercises all the authority of the first beast in his presence, and causes the earth and those who dwell in it to worship the first beast . . . Revelation 13:11,12).

I believe these symbols refer to the rise and fall of the United States of America. Let me explain why.

This lamblike beast rises out of the earth. In Revelation, the waters of the sea represent people, the sea of humanity. Other beasts, other religious and political powers, rise out of the sea. They rise out of centers of population like Europe. But this beast rises out of the earth.

This, I believe, is a picture of America rising out of the wilderness, out of a relatively uninhabited area. And this beast, unlike others, wears no crown. It has no king, no monarchy. This is the American democracy.

Also, in this gentle creature's two horns we can see a suggestion of two separate powers, church and state.

Persecuted Christians came to the wilderness of America in search of freedom of religion. They wanted to create a new society free from religious tyranny. That ideal is what has shaped the lamblike character of this country. America, Revelation suggests, would be primarily Christian by choice, by inclination.

But this image in Revelation shows us another side. This peace-loving creature, America, which looks like a lamb—ends up speaking like a dragon! The dragon is an oppressive, tyrannical figure in Revelation. In other words, the lamb starts to roar!

Why this change of character?

I see in Revelation a picture of a lamb, a good creature, taking on a dangerous kind of authority, a dangerous kind of power. It wants to enforce what it sees as good. A country with good intentions becomes oppressive and tyrannical.

And notice that it will cause the people of the world to worship the first beast. Who is that? This first beast is described in Revelation 13. It has great authority and it speaks blasphemy against God.

This is a political power that exercises religious authority. It is the ultimate false religion in the end times. And it is supported by an oppressive union of church and state. That becomes clear at the end of Revelation 13.

That lamblike creature, that lamb which roars, begins to perform great signs and wonders. It deceives many people, winning their allegiance. And then it starts to enforce the worship of this beast. It decrees that no one can buy or sell unless they have the mark or the name of the beast. Finally, it causes all who will not give the beast allegiance, to be killed.

This lamblike beast now roars like a dragon. In Revelation 13, we have a picture of a modern revival of counterfeit Christianity which uses political force to have its way in America. And it will end up enforcing the worship of a false religion.

Does it seem hard to believe that anything like that could ever happen in America? Well, consider what has been happening here at the Supreme Court. Several years ago, the Chief Justice declared that the "wall of separation between church and state is a meaningless metaphor."

And another Supreme Court Justice referred to the accommodation of diverse religious minorities as "a luxury we can no longer afford" in America.

Even more ominous is this. Just recently the Supreme Court struck down the Religious Freedom and Restoration Act. Justices reversed themselves.

Before, the government had to show a "compelling interest" if its laws interfered with the free exercise of religion. But now, the government doesn't have to demonstrate any "compelling interest."

The wall between church and state is cracking. And the church, not just the state, has been pounding away at that wall.

The wall cracks when Christians come to believe that legislating prayer in public schools is the way to save our children's souls.

The wall cracks when special-interest groups pressure legislators to enforce their religious agendas.

The wall cracks when Christians start seeing political enemies everywhere, instead of people who need Jesus everywhere.

The wall cracks when Christians mistake political influence for spiritual power.

The wall is cracking. The lamb is beginning to roar.

We have to make some very important choices as America rushes toward the year 2000. We have to make choices about what kind of power is most important. We have to make choices about who gets our ultimate allegiance.

Right now, I believe we have to take a stand against religious intolerance. I believe there is a better way than the kind of religion that is based on political power. I believe there's a better way than religion that's based on authority instead of love.

A day may soon come when Americans will have to

choose between the lamb that roars and the Lamb of God. We may have to choose between a powerful church and what the gospel is all about.

It's very important to start choosing now. Would you like to choose the Christ who built His church on love and sacrifice? Would you like to choose the power of Christ's Spirit to transform your heart?

Would you like to join me in choosing now, so that later we can stand against the tide?

Chapter 4

Let Freedom Ring!

On a cool winter day in February 1832, a young theo-
logical student was resting in his dormitory room at
Andover Seminary in Andover, Massachusetts. Samuel
Francis Smith was leafing through a sheaf of German
songs for children given him by his friend, the famed
hymnwriter and composer, Lowell Mason. As the sun set
in the western sky, painting the horizon with strokes of
crimson as from the Master Artist's brush, Smith lay on
his bed relaxing. He was exhausted from a strenuous day
of study. It was a relief to spend a few quiet moments
going over the music his friend had sent him.

As he hummed over one tune after another, one
melody above all others gripped his attention. He
hummed it again and again. He glanced at the words
at the bottom of the page and his knowledge of German
told him that the words were patriotic, but they did not
appeal to him. They lacked the inspirational quality of
all enduring music to move hearts. Samuel decided to
write his own words. He found a scrap of paper about
two and a half inches wide and five or six inches long
and began to write. On that scrap of paper, on a winter

day in the simple room of a university student, a song that would move millions was born. The words flowed freely. Samuel's pen had a hard time keeping up with his mind. It was as if some divine hand was guiding him as he wrote,

> "My country, 'tis of thee,
> Sweet land of liberty,
> Of thee I sing;
> Land where my fathers died,
> Land of the pilgrim's pride,
> From every mountainside
> Let freedom ring."

There is a yearning deep within the hearts of people everywhere for freedom. Shackled with the bonds of totalitarianism, they long to sing "sweet land of liberty." Imprisoned for the beliefs of conscience, they cry out, "let freedom ring."

In March of 1992 I conducted a massive evangelistic series preaching Christ in the citadel of Communism—the Kremlin Palace in Moscow's Red Square. Each evening I looked out on the vast sea of thousands of ordinary Russians longing for the freedom to worship God according to the dictates of conscience. The one thing that impressed me most as I stood up to speak each evening was the rapt attention of the audience. They were longing for hope. They were longing for liberty. They were longing for freedom.

I began conducting Bible-based, Christ-centered evangelistic meetings in Eastern Europe in 1986 throughout Poland, Hungary, Yugoslavia, and the former Soviet Union. The scenes of the fall of Communism are deeply etched within my memory. I well remember the events of 1989—the euphoria when the Berlin Wall came down—the dancing in the streets of East Germany— the reunions of loved ones separated for the 40 years of Communism.

The winds of change blew across Europe in the late 80s. I was in Budapest, Hungary the very night over 100,000 people marched on the Hungarian Parliament building chanting, "Let freedom ring." The democratic principles which have served as the foundation for the United States' Declaration of Independence have inspired peoples all over the world. America, with all of its problems, has served as a model of religious freedom for the world.

The roots of freedom

Those early framers of the Declaration of Independence were guided, not by their own thoughts, but by God. When the pilgrims courageously left Europe on the Mayflower and crossed the Atlantic to the unknown world of America, they wanted to escape the totalitarian religious oppression of the past. They longed to be free from the fires of the tyranny. They longed to found a nation where they would be free to worship God and practice the religion they believed in. The framers of our Constitution made clear statements about the separation of church and state. They had seen the abuses of the system in Europe and wanted to prevent such things from happening in the nation they were forming.

In 1798, George Washington made this powerful statement regarding the separation of church and state in America,

> "Every man conducting himself as a good citizen and being accountable to God alone for his religious opinion is to be protected in worshiping the Deity according to the dictates of his own conscience."

A former United States president, Calvin Coolidge, added,

> "To live under the American Constitution is the greatest political privilege God ever gave to mankind."

Is this privilege something to be taken for granted? Should we assume since freedom is the "American way" we shall always have it? Is it possible that the drumbeat of religious persecution will be heard in our land? Where is America headed?

A vision of the future

The last book of the Bible, Revelation, provides some answers. I am going to candidly share with you what Revelation predicts is rapidly approaching. Revelation reveals that a union of church and state powers is on its way in the United States of America. Revelation clearly outlines where we are headed and the issues involved.

The essence of what it means to be human is to worship God. The animal creation does not have the capacity to intelligently praise, adore, and worship God.

Satan's final attack will be over the subject of worship. Two main characters are on center stage in Revelation— the Lamb and the dragon. Revelation 13, verse 8, describes Jesus as the "Lamb slain from the foundation of the world" to guarantee our freedom. Revelation 21 and 22 describe the New Jerusalem, the fantastic capital city of the universe descending to earth with a "pure river of water of life proceeding out of the throne of God and the Lamb" (22:1).

In verse 17 Jesus, the Lamb of God, gives this gracious invitation, "And whosoever desires, let him take of the water of life freely." Revelation 5 graphically portrays "ten thousand times ten thousand" heavenly beings freely worshiping God with all the intensity of their being around God's throne. They proclaim with one harmonious voice, "Blessing and honor, and glory and power be to him that sits on the throne and to the Lamb forever and ever!" (Revelation 5:13).

Jesus, the Lamb, never coerces. The loving, compassionate Christ freely gives His life for us. His only weapon is the weapon of love. He draws us with kindness. He entices us with mercy. He attracts us with caring concern.

In contrast with the gentle invitations of the Lamb, the dragon coerces conformity. The dragon compels worship. The forces of evil in the last bitter conflict will "make war with the Lamb" (Revelation 17:14). Throughout the prophecies of Revelation, the dragon is a symbol of Satan.

Since Jesus is no longer on earth, how does Satan make war with Him? What is this war over? What is the heart of this great controversy between good and evil, and how does America fit in?

The issues are quite clearly defined in Revelation 12:17, KJV: "The dragon was wroth with the woman, and went to make war with the remnant of her seed, which keep the commandments of God and have the testimony of Jesus Christ."

Remember the dragon symbolizes Satan. A pure, undefiled woman represents God's church (Jeremiah 6:2; Ephesians 5:25-29). Satan is angry with the woman (the church) and makes war with the remnant of her seed. The word remnant means "one who remains." It is an expression describing those who remain faithful to God in earth's final days. It is an expression that describes the last part of God's church—the church in our day. And why is Satan so angry? God's people freely keep His commandments.

The importance of laws

These commandments are not some harsh, exacting, legalistic requirements. They are commands given by a loving God to ensure our freedom. When God wrote the Ten Commandments on tables of stone, His finger wrote freedom. Each of His commands is an open door to freedom—freedom to live lives of integrity, honesty, purity, kindness, unselfishness—freedom to have a joyous relationship with God and harmonious, happy relationships with one another.

From the beginning of Satan's rebellion in heaven, the Law of God has been the target of his anger. It has been the object of his wrath. Millenniums ago in heaven, he asserted his authority when he declared, "I will exalt my throne above the stars of God" (Isaiah

14:13). Kings execute their nation's law from their throne. Satan claimed God was unfair and unjust. He claimed God's law restricted the freedom of heavenly beings. The heart of the matter was simply this—Satan charged God with restricting the freedom and ultimate happiness of the heavenly beings. He used this same tactic in Eden when he suggested to Eve that if she would eat of the tree of knowledge of good and evil she would "be like God" (Genesis 3:5). His argument was that God's law restricts freedom.

Heart obedience to God's law reveals an inner allegiance. Obedience to God's law is an external manifestation of an inner faith. Obedience says, "God, I trust you. Your way is best. I have confidence to believe you know what is best for my life." Faith is accepting God's ways rather than pursuing my own. Faith is believing what God says, even when it doesn't seem to make sense. Faith is using my God-given freedom of choice to place my will on the side of right. Faith is believing God loves me and will never do me any harm. Faith leads me to obediently trust Him even when I don't understand.

Faithful obedience to God's law has been the target of Satan's anger throughout the centuries. It still will be in the final conflict. The issues in earth's last war, the issues which will be the centerpiece of religious freedom in the last days in America revolve around worship, obedience, and the commandments.

True and false worship

In Revelation chapter 14, Jesus reveals to the aged disciple John, exiled on the island of Patmos, His final warning message to the world. This urgent, vital message is to speedily go to "every nation, tribe, tongue and people" (verse 6). It calls all men and women everywhere to moral responsibility in the light of the judgment. In this passage (Revelation 14:7-12), God contrasts true and false worship. In verse 7 our Lord urges us to "worship him who made heaven and earth and the sea and springs of water" (Revelation 14:7). In verse 9 our Lord warns us against worshiping "the beast and his image." Two worships are brought into sharp, contrasting focus—worshiping the Creator and worshiping the beast. Here true and false worship are clearly delineated.

God will have a group of faithful believers who are charmed by His love. They respond to His gracious invitation. They cheerfully worship Him. They acknowledge Him as their Creator, their Redeemer, their Lord and their King. This faithful group of obedient Christians are pictured in Revelation 14:12: "Here is the patience of the saints, here are those who keep the commandments of God and the faith of Jesus."

Here are the crucial issues in earth's final conflict,

1. True worship—worshiping the Creator (verse 7).
2. False worship—worshiping the beast (verse 9).
3. Obedience—keeping the commandments (verse 12).

The entire basis of all worship is the fact that God created us (Revelation 4:11). We did not evolve. We did not create ourselves. He is worthy of our praise. He is worthy of our deepest adoration. He is worthy of our worship precisely because He is our Creator. This is why the idea of evolution is so devastating. It destroys the very essence of worship. If life simply evolved as the result of fortuitous chance, why worship at all? If we are merely the accidental happening of the right chemical formula coming together by chance over millions of eons, there is no rational reason to worship.

In this age of scientific humanism and godless evolution, God has left a timeless memorial of His creative power. This memorial is the heart of true worship. It has linked God as the Creator to His people from the beginning of time. It reveals true worship in contrast to false worship. It reveals the very reason we worship in the first place. This memorial stands as a bulwark against evolution. It stands as a monument of obedience to God. It was given by God for all mankind in the Garden of Eden. Moses describes it in the second chapter of Genesis with these words: "Thus the heavens and the earth, and all the host of them, were finished. And on the seventh day God ended His work which He had done, and He rested on the seventh day from all His work which He had done. Then God blessed the seventh day and sanctified it because in it He rested from all His work which God had created and made" (Genesis 2:1-3).

The seventh-day Sabbath was given by God at Creation to the entire human race, to all people everywhere as an everlasting memorial of His creative love and power. It is a perpetual reminder that we are His. We did not evolve. We were created by an all-knowing, incredibly loving, awesomely powerful God.

The Sabbath memorial is deeply embedded in the heart of the Ten Commandments. It is enshrined within God's law as a symbol of the reason why we worship. The fourth commandment emphatically declares, "Remember the Sabbath day to keep it holy."

The worthies of the Old Testament remembered. Abraham kept God's commandments (Genesis 26:5). The Israelites kept the Sabbath even before the law was given on Mount Sinai (Exodus 16). Isaiah, Jeremiah, Ezekiel, and Daniel were all faithful Sabbath keepers. They remembered. The apostles remembered. Peter, James, and John were Sabbath keepers. Paul preached to Jews and Gentiles on the Sabbath (Acts 13:42-44). He met privately with believers near Philippi on Sabbath (Acts 16:13). These early Christians were faithfully following Jesus' instruction, "If you love me, keep my commandments."

Jesus, our example, the model of our faith, "as His custom was went into the synagogue on the Sabbath day" (Luke 4:16). Jesus declared Himself the Lord of the Sabbath (Mark 2:27, 28; Luke 6:5; Matthew 12:8).

An eternal symbol

This is why Satan hates the Sabbath so much. The Sabbath is the eternal symbol of freely worshiping Jesus Christ as Creator, Redeemer, and Lord. It is the symbol of freedom of worship, and freedom of worship is the heart of the long-standing controversy between good and evil. Freedom of worship is the essence of Satan's final attack in the last days.

It takes moral courage to stand for truth when most people are conforming to the norms of society around them. It takes spiritual conviction to be different. It's easier to just go along with the crowd—to fade into the scenery. It's easier not to make any waves.

No, it is not always safe to follow the crowd. To have

followed the crowd in Noah's day would have meant being drowned in the Flood. To have followed the public mood in Jesus' day would have been to reject Him. To have followed the popular teachings in the Middle Ages would have meant participating in burning faithful Christian martyrs at the stake.

Why are we so afraid of taking a stand? Why are we so terrified at being different? Where is the passionate conviction of the heroes of the past? Whatever happened to the convictions of conscience that lead us to take a stand? If in this relative time of peace we are too cowardly to stand for truth, what will we do in earth's final hour when the "beast power" compels counterfeit worship? What will we do when enormous pressure is brought to bear? What will we do when we can't buy or sell? What will we do when we are faced with imprisonment and even death itself?

Truth still penetrates human hearts. It still burns its way into human minds. It still arouses men and women to action. God is still calling men and women to take a stand. God is still arousing men and women to action. Revelation's message appeals to this generation, "Worship him who made heaven and earth" (Revelation 14:7).

The foundation of true worship

The Sabbath stands at the foundation of true worship. It is a test of our willingness to serve God. You can only imagine how Satan hates the Sabbath because it is a sign of our relationship with God. It is a perpetual memorial of our freedom of worship, and Satan does not want us to be free.

George Vandeman, speaker emeritus and founder of the *It Is Written* telecast, tells a delightful story that clearly illustrates this point.

Back in the old days on the shores of the Mississippi, Abraham Lincoln stood near the market for slave trading. He watched the tragic sight of families being torn apart. Their heartbreaking sobs pierced his soul. Clenching his fists, he vowed, "If I ever get a chance at this, I will hit it hard." And he did!

Before Lincoln's great emancipation proclamation, a slave named Joe was shoved on the auction block. Bitter and resentful, he muttered, "I won't work! I won't work!" But a wealthy landowner purchased him anyway. He led Joe to the carriage, and they drove out of town to the plantation. There by a lake stood a little bungalow with curtains, flowers, and a cobblestone walkway. The new master stopped the carriage. Turning to Joe, he smiled. "Here's your new home. You don't have to work for it. I have bought you to set you free. For a moment Joe sat stunned. Then his eyes filled with tears. Overwhelmed, he exclaimed, "Master, I'll serve you forever."

Long ago someone from a land far away looked down on this earth. He saw our bondage to Satan and heard our cry for freedom. He determined, "Some day I'll get a chance to hit that, and I'll hit it hard." And Jesus did! By His death, He set us free. Like the old slave, Joe, we, too, cry out from the depths of our hearts, "Master, I'll serve you forever."

A crisis of conscience will soon break upon our world. The final events will rapidly usher in earth's final conflict over worship. Even in liberty-loving America, our freedom will fade. Powerful forces will coerce the conscience.

Have you settled it in your soul? Is your single-minded commitment, "Master, I'll serve you forever?" Why not settle it in your mind today.

Chapter 5

When Leaders Distort the Truth

The story broke upon us like a huge thunderclap on a steamy Texas summer afternoon. It gripped America's attention. The major news networks—CNN, ABC, NBC, CBS—all featured it in prime time. News commentators, Peter Jennings and Dan Rather, discussed it extensively. CNN White House correspondent, Wolf Blitzer, gave up-to-the-minute reports. People sat riveted to their television screens. They kept their radios tuned for the latest information. This was "the story," and reporters were having a "feeding frenzy." It dominated not only the news, but conversations at the dinner table and mid-morning coffee breaks. Teachers made "the story" the subject of classroom discussions, and preachers pontificated on it from their pulpits.

Sometime in mid-January, Linda Tripp, a former White House employee now employed at the Pentagon, approached representatives for independent counsel Kenneth Starr, with some potentially damaging information regarding the President of the United States, Bill Clinton. Starr was already investigating alleged wrongdoing by the President in the so-called

"Whitewater" land deal dating back to when Clinton was governor of Arkansas. Starr was also probing into a sexual harassment charge by Paula Jones. Mrs. Jones claimed that when President Clinton was the governor of Arkansas he made improper sexual advances. While Starr was investigating the story, the name of Monica Lewinsky came up as a corroborating witness. There was some evidence that Miss Lewinsky and the President might have entered into an improper relationship also. Kenneth Starr subpoenaed Miss Lewinsky. She denied the story under oath. End of the story! Right? Wrong!

Enter Linda Tripp. Linda Tripp turned over hours of taped conversations with Monica Lewinsky to independent counsel Kenneth Starr.

In these conversations, Miss Lewinsky described in somewhat graphic detail her improper relationship with the President of the United States. On January 21, 1998, President Clinton came on national television and vehemently denied having any improper relationship with Monica Lewinsky.

For seven months these denials continued. Linda Tripp was characterized as an unstable witness. Monica Lewinsky was portrayed as an awestruck, starry-eyed, sentimental 24-year-old playing fantasy mind games. For seven months the nation wondered.

In early August, Kenneth Starr cut a deal with Miss Lewinsky. He offered full immunity—freedom from any claim of wrongdoing—for her complete, truthful testimony. Starr also subpoenaed the President. On August 17 in the White House "map room," President Clinton answered Kenneth Starr's questions. His testimony was transmitted live via cable television to the grand jury seated in the Federal Court House a few blocks away.

Shortly after his grand jury testimony, President Clinton addressed the nation. In his speech he acknowledged for the first time an "improper relationship" with Miss Lewinsky. He confessed that he had misled "people, including even my wife."

The news sent Clinton supporters reeling. Trust was broken.

Confidence was shattered. Clinton aides felt let down. Democratic leaders felt betrayed.

The issues are enormous. A national, respected leader—the most powerful man on the planet—the leader of the free world—lied under oath to the American people. A respected president misled his closest followers. He distorted the truth. He covered up his immoral behavior.

Why did he do it? Why did the President of the United States mislead the nation for seven months? Was he embarrassed by his behavior? Too embarrassed to tell the truth? Was he concerned about the shame he might bring upon his family? Was he troubled about the legal implications with an on-going investigation?

I have no doubt that each of the factors above contributed to the President's decision to mislead the nation. Still there may be a more basic reason—popularity polls. Politicians live and die by national ratings. Sophisticated pollsters provide them with up-to-the-minute information. Political decisions are regularly made on the basis of polls—what gets the votes. President Clinton was faced with a moral dilemma.

If he told the truth about an illicit affair with a female

intern at the White House, and if that affair took place in the Oval Office, the American people might lose total confidence in his decision-making ability. His ratings might plummet. His popularity might collapse. He might lose the moral authority to govern.

Truth was sacrificed on the altar of popularity. To take the moral high road might make the President unpopular. He might lose popular sentiment. If the tide turned badly enough, the Republicans might even press impeachment charges.

For the sake of popularity, deceit replaced truth on the President's agenda. Throughout the centuries, truth has often been sacrificed for popularity. Doing right yields to doing what is expedient. Moral principles are exchanged for the will of the majority.

One of America's foremost poets of yesteryear put it this way,

> Truth forever on the scaffold,
> Wrong forever on the throne—
> Yet that scaffold sways the future,
> And, behind the dim unknown,
> Standeth God within the shadow, keeping
>   watch above his own.
> —James Russell Lowell, "This Present Crisis"

Is it possible that religious leaders might fall into the same trap? Just as political power tends to dictate vision, might religious power do the same thing? Just as political leaders are tempted to compromise what is right for what is expedient, might religious leaders be subject to the same temptations? Just as a nation's leaders can be powerfully influenced by the will of the people, is it possible that religious leaders might be influenced by the will of the people? Is it possible that the will of the majority could substitute for the will of the One who really counts? Might the moral principles of God be sacrificed on the altar of conformity? To appease the masses, would religious leaders dare tamper with the commands of God?

Religious compromise

Bible prophecy reveals the amazing story. It's an incredible story. It's an intriguing story of compromise and cover up. It's a story you must be aware of. Your destiny may well depend on understanding the issues involved. America has been obsessed with the Monica Lewinsky/Bill Clinton story. The average person has spent hours feeding on every morsel of the news report. Prophecy's story is much more significant. The issues are much more profound. The compromise took place generations ago. The cover up has continued for two millennia. Truth has been distorted.

The prophecies of Daniel and Revelation reveal that shortly after the death of Jesus and the apostles, compromises would subtly enter the Christian faith. In an attempt to conform to the popular culture, to make Christianity more palatable for the majority, church leaders would yield fundamental scriptural principles.

The prophet Daniel predicted that in the early centuries of Christianity the "truth" would be "cast down to the ground" (Daniel 8:12).

The apostle Paul echoes his concerns to church leaders at Ephesus with this warning: "For I know this, that after my departure savage wolves will come in among you, not sparing the flock. Also from among yourselves men will rise up speaking perverse things, to draw away the disciples after themselves. Therefore watch, and remember" (Acts 20:29-31).

The aged apostle warned church leaders at Ephesus of two significant problems the Christian church would face in the future: The problem of persecution and the problem of compromise. Persecuting forces like vicious wolves would attack the church. The bloodstained sands of history sorrowfully speak of the truthfulness of the apostle's words.

Satan's attack on early Christianity would include both elements—persecution without and apostasy within. The apostle forcefully forecast, "from among yourselves men will rise up speaking perverse things" (verse 30).

Perverse things are things which are distorted. Dr. Jack Blanco paraphrased this passage in the *Clear Word* this way: "Even from within your own group, men will begin to teach unscriptural things and there will always be some who believe what these men say and follow them" (Acts 20:30).

Speaking of the powerful, cunning, overwhelming delusions of the enemy, the apostle describes Satan's attempts to deceive to the Thessalonian Christians: "The coming of the lawless one is according to the working of Satan, with all power, signs, and lying wonders, and with all unrighteous deception among those who perish; because they did not receive the love of the truth, that they might be saved. And for this reason God will send them a strong delusion, that they should believe a lie" (2 Thessalonians 2:9, 10).

To reject the love of the truth because it is unpopular is to open our minds to Satan's deceptions. Deceptions distort truth. Deceptions bend truth to conform with popular opinion. Deceptions are often so deadly because they are so subtle. They mix truth and error. They mingle God's word with human traditions. They blend divine commands with human opinions. False worship appears as genuine worship. Satan clouds the mind. He perverts the understanding. He distorts the thinking.

The Bible's last book, Revelation, reveals this mind-altering deception. The thirteenth chapter of Revelation details a religio-political power that compromised truth to conform to the will of the popular majority. Its popular form of worship appeals to the masses.

Adolph Hitler once said, "It is easier to deceive people with a big lie than a small one." And this is a big lie—a huge deception. It involves worship. It involves God's law. It challenges God's creative authority.

"All the world" wonders after this power (Revelation 13:3, KJV). "All who dwell on the earth will worship him, whose names have not been written in the Book of Life of the Lamb slain from the foundation of the world" (Revelation 13:8).

Worship is the central issue

The central issue in the final controversy of faith reaches deep within the essence of our being. It is worship. Revelation 14:7 calls us to worship the Creator. As we discovered in our last chapter, the seventh-day Sabbath is the eternal sign of worshiping the Creator.

The Sabbath was given to us in Eden thousands of years before the existence of the Jewish race (see Genesis 2:1-3). It was given to all people everywhere.

According to Jesus' own words, "The Sabbath was made for man" (Mark 2:27).

The Sabbath constantly draws us back to the One who made us. It is the one commandment in the entire Ten Commandment law that tells us why we willingly desire to obey God's law. He made us. He knows what's best. In attacking the Sabbath, Satan has attacked the very basis for worship. He has attacked the very heart of all obedience. The prophet Daniel concluded that a compromising religio-political power would arise and "intend to change times and law" (Daniel 7:25). The very law of God, the Ten Commandments, the moral foundation of heaven's government, would be compromised.

Did a powerful church-state union attempt to change God's law to make Christianity more popular to the masses? Were church leaders willing to distort truth to conform to popular culture?

The archives of history record a fascinating story. The Christian church not only conquered paganism, paganism subtly influenced Christianity. As Christianity moved westward from Jerusalem throughout the Roman Empire, Christianity not only conquered Rome, Rome conquered Christianity. A marriage occurred between Christianity and certain elements of paganism. Statues, images, and religious icons gradually slipped into the church. Idol-worshiping pagans now felt more comfortable in the church.

Ancestor worship of the ancient pagans was replaced with worship of the dead saints. The focal point in this slide into apostasy is worship.

It has to do with God's law. The prophet Daniel predicted that in the climate of a church-state union there would be an attempted change in God's law. History confirms it. Satan attacked the very heart of God's law—the Bible Sabbath—the very emblem of creative authority.

Here's how the change occurred. It began with anti-Jewish sentiment throughout the Roman Empire. In the early second century, revolts against Rome rocked Jerusalem. Bar Kochba, a Jewish revolutionary, led a series of violent uprisings against the Romans. Feelings against the Jews were running high. Many Romans considered Christianity a Jewish sect. The disciples were Jews. The first century church was composed of thousands of Jews, and Jesus himself was a Jew.

Second, thousands of pagans gave unusual reverence to the sun. The largest luminous body in the heavens was the object of worship for many.

To disassociate from the Jews and to accommodate the pagans, some church leaders were willing to compromise. They were willing to blend truth and error. In his comprehensive volume titled *The History of the Eastern Church,* Arthur B. Stanley makes this observation: "The retention of the old pagan name of Deis Solis, or sun day is in great measure owing to the union of Christian and pagan sentiment with which the first day of the week was recommended by Constantine to his subjects, pagans and Christians alike, as the venerable day of the sun" (page 189).

The change of the Sabbath occurred over an extended

period in the early centuries without any scriptural basis. Rather than commemorate the Sabbath, which in the minds of some religious leaders linked the church with Judaism, they emphasized the Resurrection. The Resurrection nicely coincided with the pagans' reverence of the sun god on the first day of the week. As a result, with absolutely no scriptural authority, a change in the day of worship was made from the seventh-day Sabbath, Saturday, to the first day of the week, Sunday.

Here are some significant statements which confirm this fact.

"But you may read the Bible from Genesis to Revelation and you will not find a single line authorizing the sanctification of Sunday. The scriptures enforce the religious observance of Saturday, a day which we never sanctify"(Cardinal Edward Gibbons, *Faith of Our Fathers,* page 111).

"The Catholic Church for over one thousand years before the existence of a Protestant, by virtue of her divine mission, changed the day from Saturday to Sunday"(*Catholic Mirror,* September 1893).

"Question: Which is the Sabbath day?
Answer: Saturday is the Sabbath day.
Question: Why do we observe Sunday instead of Saturday?
Answer: We observe Sunday instead of

Saturday because the Catholic Church, in the Council of Laodicea (A.D. 336), transferred the solemnity from Saturday to Sunday" (Rev. Peter Geiermann, *The Convert's Catechism of Catholic Doctrine*. (See 1910 and 1948 editions).

Church leaders yielded to popular opinion. To avoid being persecuted as Jews, they compromised scriptural truth. Public sentiment for Sunday carried the day. The disciples didn't change the Sabbath. The apostle Paul emphatically declared, "Do we then make void the law through faith? Certainly not! On the contrary, we establish the law" (Romans 3:31). Jesus didn't change the Sabbath. He is "the same yesterday, today and forever" (Hebrews 13:8). God wouldn't possibly change His law. He said of himself, "I am the Lord, I do not change!" (Malachi 3:6).

A call for courage

Living on the verge of the next millennium, God is calling us to have the moral courage to stand for truth. In every individual's life God arranges circumstances for us to be confronted by the truth. On August 17, 1998, President Bill Clinton was confronted by the truth. The evidence called for a public confession and a dramatic shift in behavior.

Someone said, "America is at the crossroads." Evangelist Billy Graham amended that statement to say, "America is not at the crossroads; it is a long way down the wrong road." At a time of moral compromise, God speaks. At a time when the "majority rules" rather than "God rules," our Lord speaks. At a time of dodging the truth, evading responsibility, do your own thing, it's a personal matter, slippery slide living, God speaks. His still small voice calls us to faithfulness. His still small voice calls us to commitment. His still small voice calls us to steadfastness.

The price of compromise is just too high. President Clinton lost too much because of his illicit escapades with a young White House intern. He lost the respect of thinking, decent people all over the world. He lost the confidence of tens of thousands of supporters. He lost something—an immense amount—in the intimate circle of his family. He may lose his presidency. The price of moral compromise is just too high.

This reality is not only true with the President of the United States, it's also true with every citizen of the United States. It's true with you and it's true with me. To sell out truth simply to be popular is a colossal error.

There is One whose commitment to truth led His blood-stained feet up Golgotha's hill. His commitment to His Father's will led Him to willingly open His fists, laying bare His palms as muscular, strong-armed Roman soldiers smashed rusty, jagged spikes through His hands. There is One who faced the hiding of the Father's face to do the Father's will. There is One who experienced the guilt of sin to atone for the condemnation of sin. There is One who cried out from the depths of His being, "My God, my God, why have You forsaken Me?", so we could feel the Father's warm embrace. There is One who died so we could live.

This Christ invites you to make a complete, total surrender to Him today. He invites you to commit your life to Him for all eternity. Why not bow your head right now? Why not settle it in your heart today before you

read the next chapter? Why not pray the simple prayer
of the hymnwriter right now?

> "I will follow Thee, my Saviour,
> Wheresoe'er my lot may be.
> Where Thou goest I will follow;
> Yes, my Lord, I'll follow Thee.
> I will follow Thee, my Saviour,
> Thou didst shed Thy blood for me;
> And though all men should forsake Thee,
> By Thy grace I'll follow Thee."
> —James Lawson

Chapter 6

The Pope Calls for Sunday Observance

On May 31, 1998, Pope John Paul II issued an urgent appeal to the bishops, clergy, and faithful of the Catholic Church for a revival of Sunday observance. His lengthy forty-page pastoral letter makes a passionate plea for greater attendance at Sunday Mass.

In this appeal, the Pope is extremely concerned that attendance at Sunday Mass is "strikingly low." He believes the future of the Catholic Church and society in general will be threatened if decisive steps are not taken. The Pope's answer—rest and worship on Sunday. The significance of his letter is enormous. The implications are shocking. For Bible-believing Christians there are storm clouds on the horizon.

After carefully delineating what he believes are the biblical, sociological, and cultural arguments in favor of Sunday, the Pope discusses the State's obligation to guarantee a worker's right to Sunday worship. He says:

In this matter my predecessor, Pope Leo XIII, in his Encyclical *Rerum Novarum* spoke of

Sunday rest as a worker's right which the *State must guarantee.*

In our historical context, there remains *the obligation* to ensure that everyone can enjoy the freedom, rest, and relaxation which human dignity requires together with the associated religious, family, cultural and interpersonal needs which are difficult to meet if there is no guarantee of at least one day of the week on which both people can rest and celebrate. . . .

Therefore, also in the particular circumstances of our own time, Christians will naturally strive to ensure that civil legislation respects their duty to keep Sunday holy.

The papal letter illustrates the need for "civil legislation" to keep Sunday holy with a fascinating review of history. The first civil legislation to promulgate the sanctity of Sunday was passed by the Roman emperor Constantine in A.D. 321. Prior to this, Sunday observance was not protected by civil legislation. Professor Samuele Bacchiocchi of Andrews University makes this significant observation:

In many cases Christians would attend an early morning service [on Sunday] and then spend the rest of Sunday working at their various occupations. Thus the Constantinian Sunday Law, as the Pope points out, was not 'a mere historical circumstance with no special significance for the church' but a providential protection that made it possible for Christians to observe Sunday "without hindrance."

The importance of *civil legislation* that guarantees Sunday rest is indicated by the fact that "even after the fall of the Empire the Councils did not cease to insist upon arrangements [civil legislation] regarding Sunday rest."

—Samuele Bacchiocchi, "The Pope Calls for Sunday Observance," E-mail Document, July 20, 1998 (samuele@andrews.edu)

It is fascinating that the Pope uses the Constantinian Sunday Law as a model for the future. It is significant that the Pope of Rome approaches the issue of civil legislation from the perspective of deteriorating social and moral conditions. The Pope's analogy is obvious. In the fourth century, church and state united in the Roman Empire, according to the Pope, to "ensure the freedom, rest and relaxation which human dignity requires." The Pope sees this church/state union as a model for our Sunday. He urges Christians everywhere to press for civil legislation regarding Sunday worship.

Some Protestants are heeding the call for civil legislation to protect the sanctity of Sunday as well. The moral fabric of society is falling apart. Divorce is rampant. Crime is of epidemic proportion. Drug abuse is commonplace. Sexual immorality and violence on television have become the norm. There is a powerful movement underway to restore family values in our society. We are beginning to see a backlash against the liberalism and secular humanism which have had such a strong influence in our society. Scrapping our moral values in the 60s and early 70s has led to a tragic harvest in the 80s and 90s. We have cut down the tree of Christian morality, and the fruit of Christian virtue is rotting on the withered branches of our society.

Due to these deteriorating moral values, conservative Christians have begun working to form a political base of power that can pass a new social agenda. The cover story blurb on the May 15, 1995 *Time* magazine declares, "Meet Ralph Reed, 33. His Christian Coalition is on a crusade to take over American politics and it's working."

Commenting on the need for religious organizations to work together to create a "moral society," Reed states:

> No longer burdened by the past, Roman Catholics, Evangelicals, Greek Orthodox and many religious conservatives from the denominations are forming a new alliance that promises to become the most powerful and important in the modern political era.
>
> — "Politically Incorrect," *Time* magazine, May 15, 1995, page 16.

Ralph Reed, former director of the Christian Coalition, and Pope John Paul II have something in common. One fundamental fact is driving them. The liberal, humanistic, secular approach to society is not working. Christian virtues of honesty, integrity, moral purity, kindness, self-control, and decency are at an all-time low. Something must be done before social chaos and moral anarchy steal the day. Something must be done to solve the moral crisis society faces.

Pat Robertson of the popular Christian television broadcast, The 700 Club agrees. In his book, *The New World Order*, he echoes similar thoughts to the Pope's and Ralph Reed's. Robertson observes:

> Laws in America that demanded a day of rest from incessant commerce have been nullified as a violation of church and state. In modern America, shopping centers, malls and stores of every description carry on their frantic pace seven days a week as an outright insult to God and his plan. Only those policies which have a clearly secular purpose are recognized.

Robertson argues that a godly state must have religious laws at its heart. He sees civil legislation regarding Sunday as the cohesive element that provides a moral foundation for society.

Could it be possible that the stage for religious intolerance is subtly being set? Are the Pope's pastoral letter and the growing calls from conservative Protestants a sign of what's to come? Is this the echo of fulfillment of Revelation's prophecy? Will this movement usher in a final union of church and state powers? Do we hear the drumbeat of religious persecution in the Pope's proclamation? Is there a biblical precedent that will give us scriptural insight into what's happening today?

Daniel's prophecies of our day

I believe that there is! I am convinced that the prophet Daniel wrote specifically for our time. His prophecies speak to us. They provide us with insights for our day. The twelfth chapter reveals that Daniel's prophecies are especially for us.

"But thou, O Daniel, shut up the words, and seal the book, even to the time of the end" (verse 4).

And one said to the man clothed in linen, which was above the waters of the river, "How long shall the fulfillment of these wonders be?" (verse 6).

"But you, go your way till the end: for you shall rest and will arise to your inheritance at the end of the days" (verse 13).

The book of Daniel is divided into two sections—stories and prophecies. The prophecies tell us *when*. They reveal the rise and fall of nations. They unfold the panorama of history. They describe a titanic struggle between the forces of good and evil through the centuries. The prophecies portray Satan's subtle, masterful attempts to distort truth. They unmask the plans of the enemy and reveal the plans of God.

The stories tell us *how*. They specifically reveal how to live at end time. The prophet Daniel lived to be close to ninety. A biography detailing Daniel's life could easily run 600-700 pages. Surprisingly enough, God chose to record only six specific stories in the entire book of Daniel. (1) The story of Jerusalem's fall and Daniel's captivity. (2) The story of Daniel's interpretation of the king's dream. (3) The story of the fiery furnace. (4) The story of Nebuchadnezzar's insanity. (5) The story of the fall of Babylon and (6) The story of the lions' den.

Have you ever wondered why Daniel's life is compacted into just these six stories? Why were they chosen and no others? What's significant about these six stories? Remember, the fundamental purpose of Daniel's book is for end time. It's a book for the "last days." It was given by a loving God to prepare a people for the crisis at the close. Each of these specific stories is especially crafted by God to reveal the character qualities necessary for earth's final hours. These stories especially give us insight into what is coming. This is why Daniel chapter 3 is so significant. The events of Daniel 3 form a striking parallel to those in Revelation 13.

In Daniel 3 the Babylonian king, Nebuchadnezzar, set up the golden image and compelled worship. This image is a counterfeit. God has revealed the true outline of history in chapter 2. Daniel had interpreted Nebuchadnezzar's dream of the image with the head of gold, the breast and arms of silver, the thighs of brass, the legs of iron, and the feet of iron and clay with the mysterious stone smashing the image to pieces and filling the entire earth.

Each distinct metal represented a nation. Babylon, Media-Persia, Greece, and Rome would rise in distinct succession. The prophecy predicted Rome's fall and subsequent division. According to Daniel's interpretation, the "stone cut out without hands" represented the eternal establishment of God's everlasting kingdom. Nebuchadnezzar was shocked. He wanted his kingdom to last forever. The archeologists have uncovered this inscription attributed to the Babylonian king, "O

Babylon, the delight of mine eyes, the excellency of my kingdoms. May it last forever."

The head of gold in the image of chapter 2 representing Babylon followed by the breast and arms of silver depicting Media-Persia did not fit in with Nebuchadnezzar's plans of a universal kingdom. His ambitions did not foresee the Medes and Persians triumphing over Babylon.

The golden image Nebuchadnezzar erected on the plain of Dura was a counterfeit of the one he saw in his dream in chapter 2. This new image was the Babylonian Empire. The Babylonian ruler passed a universal decree compelling worship of this counterfeit image. The edict or state law carried with it the penalty of death for all those who would not bow down. The entire nation was summoned to bow down and worship the counterfeit image. The decree was universal. The Bible phrases the king's decree in these words,

> "To you it is commanded, O people, nations and languages that at what time you hear . . . all kinds of music you shall fall down and worship the gold image that King Nebuchadnezzar has set up. And whoever does not fall down and worship shall be cast immediately into the midst of a burning fiery furnace" (Daniel 3:4-6).

The Babylonian furnaces were heated seven times hotter than normal. A powerful world leader, Nebuchadnezzar, passed a universal decree condemning to death those who would not accept counterfeit worship. The second commandment, "Thou shalt not worship graven images," became the outer sign of an inner loyalty to God. Commitment was tested by obedience. Faith was revealed in action. Daniel's friends, Shadrach, Meshach, and Abednego refused to bow down. They refused to yield their conscientious convictions to the state decree. They would not accept compelled worship. They refused the church/state enforced worship. Truth was more important than preserving a unified social order. They could not compromise their integrity for the will of the majority. The three Hebrew worthies confidently declared,

> "Our God whom we serve is able to deliver us from the burning fiery furnace, and he will deliver us from your hand, O king. But if not, let it be known to you, O king, that we will not serve thy gods, nor worship the gold image which you have set up" (Daniel 3:17, 18).

What courage! What faith! What conviction! It is highly likely that there were other Hebrews on the plain of Dura that day. It is also possible that some of them did bow down in conformity to the king's command. Why? What leads people to surrender their personal convictions for the crowd? What motivates them to compromise their integrity?

For some, it may be the fear of being different, or peer pressure. For others, it might be concern over the consequences of their actions. They are afraid of what they will lose if they stand for principle. Truth is judged in the hall of popular opinion. It is weighed in the balance scales of the consequences and the results of the decision.

Shadrach, Meshach, and Abednego, too, stared the consequences in the face and confidently moved forward. They trusted God. Lack of trust is one of the major ingredients in compromise. Their faith led them to commit to God's will at any cost. They were roughly thrown into the fiery furnace.

The king was astonished as he arrogantly viewed the scene. The Hebrews were not consumed. As the king looked into the flames, he saw a fourth being in their midst. Immediately he sensed that this fourth being was the Son of God. The divine Protector, the Lord Jesus Christ, was with His people in their time of greatest trial.

The story of the three Hebrew worthies is much more than a general story of divine protection. It applies with special force to the end time. It has a powerful last-day application. The Bible's last book, Revelation, reveals that once again in the last days of earth's history a counterfeit image will be established—a substitute sign of allegiance, a false mark of loyalty. According to Revelation 13:12, the issue once again will be worship. Revelation 14:6 clearly calls all men and women on planet Earth to worship the Creator in contrast to worshiping the beast.

Revelation describes two leaders—the Lamb and the dragon. It describes two cities—spiritual Jerusalem, the citadel of truth, and spiritual Babylon, the citadel of apostasy. It describes two worships—worshiping the Creator and worshiping the beast. It describes two unions—the Christian union with Christ and a church/state union. It describes two philosophies—the freedom to worship in harmony with the dictates of individual conscience and coerced worship which universally attempts to force individuals to conform to the will of the majority.

In Daniel 3 at a time of a powerful church/state union and coerced worship, the three Hebrews chose the way of obedience rather than the way of compromise. By faith they kept the commandments of God. Faith always leads to obedience, never disobedience.

Is it possible that the Pope's decree to establish Sunday through civil legislation is part of the larger picture of the fulfillment of Revelation's prophecies? Is it possible that the "religious right" might unite with Roman Catholics to enforce Sunday observance to save a society on the brink of moral collapse? Is it possible that America's religious freedom could be eroded for the "good of the majority" at a time of serious moral crisis? Would the average American accept subtle constitutional changes if they thought it might bring America back to its godly roots? Would the average person accept the directions of an authority figure contrary to their own feelings of right if they felt the authority figure's directions served a higher good?

Compelling Conscience

Dr. Stanley Milgram, a psychologist, conducted experiments to discover just how far a person will go in causing pain to another individual when he is ordered to do so. His experiments contain significant lessons for those of us living at end time. The results of these studies are not only extremely significant, but mighty frightening.

The experiments were conducted some years ago at

Yale University. Advertisements were placed in New Haven, Connecticut, newspapers asking for 500 male volunteers to participate in a study of memory. As men responded, appointments were set up. When a volunteer arrived at the laboratory for his appointment, a second man would arrive at the same time, posing as another volunteer. Actually, the second man was an actor hired to help with the experiment.

The two men were told that they were participating in a study of the effects of punishment on learning. One was to be the teacher and the other the learner. They were allowed to draw to see which role each would play, but the drawing was rigged so that the actor would always play the role of the learner. The teacher and learner were in separate rooms, but the teacher could observe that the learner was hooked up to what seemed to be an electrode. The teacher was instructed to administer an electric shock to the learner whenever he made a mistake, and to increase the voltage with each new mistake.

The actor, who played the part of the student, would not actually receive any shocks at all, but when the "teacher" raised the voltage dial to 75 volts, he would act like he had been mildly hurt. At 120 volts he would begin to complain, and at 150 volts he would demand that the experiment cease. If the "teacher" continued to administer shocks, at 285 volts the actor would let out an agonized scream.

Many "teachers" would begin to protest when they realized they were injuring another person, but would be ordered to go on because the experiment must continue. Many of them would continue giving shocks up to the highest levels, no matter how much the actor begged to be released.

Now you may think that anybody in his or her right mind wouldn't even give the first shock, but the terrible truth is that almost two-thirds of the participants were willing to go to almost any length when commanded to do so. Many went all the way up to 450 volts, no matter how hard the victim begged to be released. Why did they do it? Did they want to? No. Was it because of the aggressiveness or hostility in their nature? No. They did it simply because a man in a laboratory coat told them to do it. That white coat represented to them authority. No police badge, no gun, just a white coat.

The volunteers were interviewed afterward and asked why they had continued giving the shocks. Almost invariably the answer was the same—it was simply that they had been ordered to do it. Many believed that what they were doing was very wrong, but they didn't have the courage to refuse to go on. By the time the experiment was over, they had justified their conduct on the basis that they were simply following orders. They were more concerned about how good a job they had done.

Why didn't they just walk out if they thought it was wrong? Simple reasons—they wanted to be polite. They were helping science. They had made a commitment. It would be awkward.

Yes, it is very awkward to disobey an order. And I wonder if you see the frightening implications. The horrors of Nazi Germany were not all committed by a man named Hitler. They were carried out by subordinates at all levels who were just following orders. Even the notorious Eichman, who was sickened when he visited the gas chambers, insisted that he was just a man at a desk shuffling papers and following orders.

Here is the precise issue in the long-standing controversy between good and evil. The essence of God's image revealed in His children is free will—the ability to choose. God does not coerce His children. He does not force them to worship Him. A gracious God lovingly invites. He gently appeals. All coercion, force, and pressure is contrary to the government of God. The "teachers" in Dr. Milgram's experiment at Yale University surrendered their ability to choose. They obeyed another whom they considered to be an authority figure. They allowed someone else to shape their moral decisions. Someone else controlled their minds.

Time is running out. The stage is being set. The forces of intolerance will soon be released. The persecutions of the past will be repeated. Conscientious, Bible-believing Christians will be imprisoned for their faith. Our religious liberty one day will fade away.

When the crisis finally breaks upon this world, God will have a group of people who are loyal and true. Like the three Hebrew worthies, they will choose to serve God. Their faith will extend beyond the flames. It will soar heavenward to the eternal throne. By faith they will picture their coming King—when the furnace is heated seven times hotter—when a time of trouble greater than any previous time of trouble in history rocks the earth—God's people will hang on. They know their Savior is returning. Through the flames of life, they will see His face. Persecuted and oppressed, they will cling to His promises. They will sing in the darkness. They will praise God in the night of their trial. They are His. No one can take them out of His hand. No demon of hell or oppressive power on earth can snuff out their lives. They belong to Him. They are safe. They can sing with the hymnwriter,

> Safe in the arms of Jesus,
> Safe on His gentle breast.
> Here by His love o'er shaded,
> Sweetly my soul doth rest.
> —Fanny J. Crosby

Chapter 7

The Future of the American Dream

On April 26, 1607, colonist George Percy reported his first glimpse of the New World. He described landing near the James River among "faire meddowes and goodly tall trees, with such fresh-waters running through the woods, as I was almost ravished at the first sight thereof."

George and his fellow colonists would move their ships up the river to a well protected spot and build crude huts and fortifications. Jamestown would become their flower-covered foothold on this continent.

The American Dream had begun.

Another colonist, John Smith, had been quite an adventurer in Europe. He was celebrated for his heroic feats against Turkish warriors in single-handed combat. But here in this settlement, he found an even greater adventure.

Smith, more than anyone else, promoted America to his countrymen back in England, as a great, natural garden, a paradise. Speaking of this area of Virginia, he wrote, "heaven and earth never agreed better to frame a place for man's habitation."

In America, John Smith saw limitless possibilities.

So did his friend, John Rolfe. He was the first to show the settlers at Jamestown how to grow profitable crops. This devout Puritan felt that he and his fellow colonists were on a divine mission—like the Israelites entering the Promised Land.

Rolfe wrote this to the King of England: "What need have we then to fear, but to go up at once as a peculiar people marked and chosen by the finger of God to possess it? For undoubtedly he is with us."

This man found a mission in the New World. He also found true love. Rolfe became greatly attached to the Indian princess, Pocahontas, while she was in Jamestown. He wrote a touching letter to the governor asking permission to marry the woman "to whom my heart is and best thoughts are . . . so entangled."

Pocahontas studied the Bible with a Puritan minister and accepted the Christian faith. Rolfe and Pocahontas were married and sailed back to England, where the bride made quite a sensation at the royal court.

The American Dream had taken on a whole new meaning for John Rolfe. But soon that dream would crash against some harsh realities.

Some dreams have a way of colliding against reality. That's what happened to John Rolfe, the visionary colonist who married Pocahontas.

Tragically, less than a year after the happy couple reached England, Pocahontas died, probably of tuberculosis. John Rolfe returned to Jamestown to try to find a purpose again. But Jamestown was beginning to change.

The idealism of the first settlers was fading. Their dream of "a city set on a hill" was being replaced by get-rich-quick schemes. Jamestown became a settlement of transients. By the 1640s, many of the colonists were drinking themselves into a stupor. That, in fact, was their principal means of recreation and relaxation.

Innkeepers were cheating and overcharging their guests. The public houses were filled with what was referred to as "idleness and debauchery." Gambling became a real concern. Sometimes plantation owners could be seen putting up their servants as stakes in a game.

The American Dream had been a spiritual quest for many of the early settlers. But that dream couldn't always be sustained. In Jamestown it faded among all the drunks lying in the mud of the once-brave settlement.

The American Dream

The fate of Jamestown makes us ponder the American Dream today. This country was founded on great ideals, on liberty, democracy and the dignity of the individual. Many of the people who built America had very strong spiritual and moral values.

But the American Dream is in danger of dying.

In Washington, just a few blocks from the White House, there are streets haunted by crime, drug addiction, and chronic poverty. Sometimes our country doesn't seem to be holding together anymore. Gangs are tearing neighborhoods apart. Corruption in government makes us more and more cynical. And racial tensions still divide us.

What is happening to the American Dream that men like Washington, Jefferson, and Lincoln worked so hard to nurture? Where is this country going? Can we ever capture that sense of noble destiny again?

People in America have many questions today about the future.

Can we make our streets safe again? Or will gangs keep taking over more and more turf?

Will the family keep fracturing in America, or will we find some way to save it?

America has always been a fortress of religious liberty, of freedom of expression. Will those basic freedoms last, or will bigotry and coercion replace them?

Is America, the Melting Pot, gone for good? Will the races continue to polarize, or will we find a way to see eye-to-eye?

And what about the church? Will secular forces eventually overwhelm Christianity?

What is going to happen to America in the next millennium? What is going to happen to the American Dream? These are questions that haunt us all.

I'd like to suggest that we can find some answers today in a place you may not have looked. It's surprising how many of our questions and concerns are actually addressed in the Bible, especially in the book of Revelation. This is a revelation about the future. And it's a revelation about how Jesus Christ is going to be there in our future.

The prophecies in this book deal with the future of the American Dream. They give us a picture of where this country, and the world in general, is heading. So let's take a look.

Revelation's vision of the future

First of all, Revelation is a book of startling contrasts. It shows us terrible plagues. And it shows us glorious, heavenly worship. It shows us horrifying beasts. And it shows us angelic creatures.

Revelation pictures the future, our future, in stark contrasts. Let's look at some examples.

What's the future of the Christian church? Look at the picture in Revelation 19. The church is symbolized by a pure woman. She prepares herself for marriage with Christ, the Lamb of God. " 'Let us be glad and rejoice and give Him [God] glory, for the marriage of the Lamb has come, and His wife has made herself ready.' And to her it was granted to be arrayed in fine linen, clean and bright, for the fine linen is the righteous acts of the saints" (Revelation 19:7, 8).

This is a beautiful picture of the future of the church. Everyone is rejoicing. The church has made herself ready for Christ. She is clothed with fine linen, a bright garment that represents the transforming righteousness of Christ. The godly lives of Christians fill the church with compassion and justice and genuine worship.

But there's another picture in Revelation too, another picture of the future, another woman, a harlot who sits on a scarlet beast.

"The woman was arrayed in purple and scarlet, and adorned with gold and precious stones and pearls, having in her hand a golden cup full of abominations and the filthiness of her fornication" (Revelation 17:4).

This woman is called Babylon, the Mother of Harlots. She deceives all nations by her sorcery. She is a habitation of demons, a prison for every foul spirit.

In contrast to the bride of Christ, this woman represents a false religious system, a system allied with the political power of the dragon who speaks blasphemy.

This false religious system seduces many people. It causes individuals all over the world to worship the antichrist, to worship the beast.

That's the other picture of our future.

What is going to happen to Christianity? One picture shows us great rejoicing over a pure woman clothed with righteous deeds. The other picture shows us a harlot who seduces and degrades.

A divided church

What is Revelation telling us? It's telling us that in the difficult times ahead the Christian church is going to go in two totally different directions. When times get tough, we will go one way or the other. Part of the church will make herself ready spiritually for union with Christ. Part of the church will become a habitation of demons.

What a contrast!

Paul echoes this same idea. He tells us very clearly in First Timothy:

"Now the Spirit expressly says that in latter times some will depart from the faith, giving heed to deceiving spirits and doctrines of demons, speaking lies in hypocrisy, having their own conscience seared with a hot iron" (1 Timothy 4:1, 2).

Here's a group of believers who trade the truths of Scripture for the doctrines of demons. It's a terrible picture of the church corrupted in the last days.

And yet, again, Revelation gives us a contrasting picture. It shows us a faithful "remnant" of believers in the end times. Revelation identifies the group in this way:

"Here is the patience of the saints; here are those who keep the commandments of God and the faith of Jesus" (Revelation 14:12).

Here's the church getting ready for that marriage with the Lamb. People are clinging to God's word, to His commandments. They are living their lives according to principle. And they are centering their lives around faith in Jesus Christ. They stand in stark contrast to those whose consciences are seared with a hot iron.

In the book of Revelation, the church is going in opposite directions. Christians are going in opposite directions. That's what awaits us in the future.

The lamb-like beast in Revelation 13 speaks like a dragon. We know reasons why this beast represents America. Revelation 13 further tells us just what role this beast will play in the end times.

Incredibly enough, scripture clarifies that America is going to be part of an oppressive system of false religion. It is pictured making an image of a terrible beast that speaks blasphemy against God. It coerces people into worshiping this image. Revelation 13 tells us it uses economic pressure. No one can buy or sell unless they have the mark of the beast. And finally, it causes all who won't worship the beast to be killed.

This is a terrible picture of America in the future. How is such a thing possible? Because part of the church sells out, part of the church becomes a habitation of demons, part of the church becomes a harlot.

But again, there's another picture in Revelation, another picture of believers standing tall, of the church uncorrupted.

"And they overcame him [that is the dragon, or Satan] by the blood of the Lamb and by the word of their testimony, and they did not love their lives to the death." Revelation 12:11).

We have believers who cave in. But we also have believers who overcome. How? By the blood of the Lamb. They're focused on Christ and His sacrifice for them. They're devoted to Christ. That's what they talk about. That's what they're willing to give their lives for.

Revelation is a book of startling contrasts. It's a book of horror and of glory. And that's what awaits us in the future in America.

What is going to happen to the family? It's going to be attacked even more fiercely. The love of many will grow cold, basic bonds will be destroyed.

And yet the family will be preserved stronger than ever—by a group that honors God's commandments and preserves the faith of Jesus.

What is going to happen to traditional values? They're going to be trampled. In the last days, Paul tells us, individuals will despise the good, grow headstrong and haughty, and lack all self-control.

And yet others remain undefiled, in their mouth is no guile. They stand without fault before the throne of God.

What is going to happen to our political system? Will it become a tool of religious tyranny? Will the lamb of America, the champion of religious freedom, roar like a beast? Will it try to enforce false worship?

The Bible reveals that many will refuse to worship

the beast. They will give their lives "for their witness to Jesus and for the word of God." They will make history's most glorious stand for freedom.

What is going to happen to the American Dream? It's going to turn to ashes in the hands of those who refuse to love the truth, those who become so blinded that they can actually worship a beast of blasphemy. Revelation 9 pictures them. Even after the final plagues begin to fall they still keep on worshiping demons and idols. They're still trapped in sexual immorality and theft and sorcery and murder.

And yet for others, the American Dream is going to be realized in a way much more glorious than we have imagined. It's going to come true in a way the settlers of Jamestown couldn't have imagined—even when they looked at the unspoiled beauty of a new continent.

When we look out over the city of Washington, we are captured by the vision of those who laid out this city as the capital of democracy, the capital of freedom. From a distance, the American Dream can still seem very real.

Final dream

Well, let me take you to the final great dream, the final great vision of the author of the book of Revelation, the Apostle John. Because he saw, in the future, a glorious city descending to earth, a city which would become the capital of grace and love on earth, the capital of God's glory. John called it the New Jerusalem. In his vision he saw heaven coming down to earth.

The American Dream of people like John Smith and John Rolfe was more than just a prosperous plantation. It was also a spiritual quest. And I hope that the American Dream for us is more than just a nice house in the suburbs.

The real American Dream is about being a chosen people who find our place in the world, a people who conquer new territory in the name of Christ, a people who are captured by a divine mission, a mission of bringing heaven down to earth.

That's what Jesus Christ is going to do someday. That's the climax of the book of Revelation, the Second Coming of Christ.

The Apostle John saw it in a vision. He saw the sky split open and the King of Kings descend like a conqueror on a white horse.

He saw the Holy City, the New Jerusalem, coming down out of heaven from God, looking like a beautiful bride.

He saw God shining like the sun in this city.

He saw a new heaven and a new earth.

He saw God wiping every tear from our eyes.

He saw a river of life, clear as crystal, flowing from the throne of God.

He saw a multitude from every country on earth circling God's throne, waving palm branches, lifting up their voices in exuberant praise.

This is what John saw. This is the New Earth Dream. This is how the kingdom of God becomes a reality in this world. This is the ultimate solution for broken families and crime-ridden streets. The American Dream can only be fulfilled in John's New Earth Dream.

As America rushes toward the year 2000, we will be facing some hard choices. Difficult times will push us in two very different directions. Some will be seduced by a false religious system. Some will be blinded and come to believe in the doctrines of demons. Some will become part of a tyranny more horrifying than they can imagine.

But others will overcome these dark forces. They will stand firm for freedom and justice and love. And these people are distinguished by one thing in the book of Revelation: their devotion to Christ. They are overwhelmed by the value of His sacrifice. They can't stop singing His praises: "Worthy is the Lamb that was slain." They are said to follow Him wherever He goes. Their robes are made white in the blood of the Lamb.

And these are the people who will welcome Christ at His second coming. These are the people who will inhabit the New Jerusalem. These are the people who will see the New Earth Dream come true.

Don't you want to be part of that glorious climax of history? Your deepest dreams, your most secret longings can come true in the future that God has planned. It's the real fulfillment of the American Dream. It's the real fulfillment of your dreams.

Please make a commitment right now to follow the Lamb wherever He goes. Make a commitment to Jesus Christ as the way, the truth, and the life. He is the only place of security in the days ahead. He will see you safely through to that day when heaven comes down to earth.